A New True Book

FARM ANIMALS

By Karen Jacobsen

*This "true book" was prepared
under the direction of
Illa Podendorf,
formerly with the Laboratory School,
University of Chicago*

 CHILDRENS PRESS, CHICAGO

PHOTO CREDITS

Art Thoma Photo—2

James P. Rowan—14 (right), 17, 23 (bottom), 30, 34, 35, 42 (2 photos)

Lynn M. Stone—13, 20 (2 photos), 23 (top), 43

USDA (United States Department of Agriculture)—4, 6, 8, 9, 10, 14 (left), 15, 18 (2 photos), 24, 25, 28 (2 photos), 31, 32, 36 (top), 38, 44 (2 photos), 45

Texas State Department of Highways & Public Transportation—27, 36 (bottom), 40, 41

Library of Congress Cataloging in Publication Data

Jacobsen, Karen.
  Farm animals.

  (A New true book)
  SUMMARY: Briefly describes some of the most com-
mon farm animals: chickens, cows, pigs, sheep,
goats, and horses.
  1. Domestic animals—Juvenile literature.
[1. Domestic animals]   I. Title.
SF75.5.J32   1981   636   81-7686
ISBN 0-516-01619-9   AACR2

TABLE OF CONTENTS

"ERR-er-ERR-er-ERRR!"
the rooster crows and
wakes up everybody.
The sun is rising.
A new day is here.
"ERR-er-ERR-er-ERRR!"

CHICKENS

It is morning on the chicken farm.

All of the chickens are awake. They are very hungry.

Chickens eat grain and
other seeds. They eat corn.
But they have no teeth
to chew their food. Instead
they swallow tiny stones.
The stones help to grind
up their food.

Hens lay eggs. They sit on the eggs to keep them warm.

In three weeks the eggs will break open. Baby chicks will come out. The mother hen will take care of her chicks.

Baby chicks eat baby chick food. It helps them to grow strong and healthy.

In six weeks the chicks will be able to eat grain and other seeds—just like the big chickens.

Chickens have wings and tails and beaks and claws. They are covered with feathers.

Chickens are always looking for food. They keep busy all day long.

COWS

The day starts early on a dairy farm.

The cows are all awake. They are standing outside the barn. The cows are waiting to be milked.

There are milking
machines inside the barn.
The milking machines are
easy to use. These
machines help to keep the
milk clean.

Milk is very important. It has many uses.

Milk is used to make food, such as butter, cream, and ice cream.

Milk is also used to make glue, paint, and plastics.

After milking, the cows go out to pasture. There they eat lots of sweet grass. They swallow the grass quickly.

Later the grass comes back into their mouths. This time they chew it very carefully. Then they swallow the grass and it gets into their stomachs.

Guernsey cow

Baby cows are called "calves."

Calves stay with their mothers. They drink their mother's milk for six months. Then they start to eat grass—just like their mothers.

Cows stay in the pasture all day.

They eat grass and they drink water. Sometimes they lick salt from a salty block.

Late in the afternoon the cows go back to the barn. It is time for a second milking.

PIGS

On hot days pigs roll in the mud. They are not trying to get dirty. They are helping themselves.

Pigs cannot sweat the way people do. They cover their skins with mud. It keeps them cool.

Baby pigs are called "piglets."

Usually many piglets are born at one time. The mother pig spends lots of time caring for her babies.

Usually 6, 8 or more piglets are born at one time.

Pigs eat grain and special pig food. They eat a lot. But they do not eat too much.

Pigs grow big and get very heavy. Some weigh over 1000 pounds.

SHEEP

Sheep stay together.
All day long they
eat grass out in the fields.
At night they stay together
under the stars.

During the winter sheep grow thick wool coats. The wool protects them from rain and snow. It keeps them warm.

In early summer the wool is cut off the sheep. The sheep are not hurt. They start to grow a new wool coat right away.

Sheep's wool is made into yarn. The yarn is used to make clothes to keep people warm.

There is oil in sheep's wool. The oil is made into many things that we use every day.

Baby sheep are called "lambs."

Lambs are very cute. They jump and play all day.

Most of the time they stay close to their mothers.

GOATS

Goats are very curious. They climb up high to see what they can see.

Some goats have thick
wool coats like sheep.
Other goats have short,
shiny hair.

Goats give milk. Their milk is made into rich cheese.

Goats eat grass, green leaves, bark, and twigs. They also eat clover, apples, carrots, and other good things that they find. Goats make good lawn mowers.

HORSES

Once horses were very important on farms. They helped farmers to clear and plow fields. They worked hard.

LIVERY BARN

On ranches cowboys still ride horses and herd cattle.

Horses can run fast and carry heavy loads.

Horses are strong and fast. But now tractors and trucks do most of the work on farms.

Today people ride horses for fun.

Horses eat hay and oats and other grains. Sometimes they eat carrots or apples.

Horses need lots of care.

They must be brushed every day.

They need fresh water to drink.

They need to live in clean places.

Horses like to be
outside. They need lots of
room to run.

FARM ANIMALS ARE FUN

Farm animals are fun to watch.
Horses run.

Goats climb.

Sheep eat grass.

Pigs keep cool.

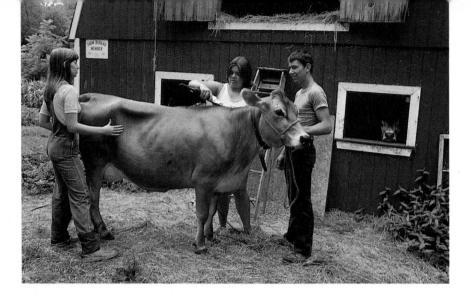

Cows give milk.

Chickens look for food.

Farm animals keep busy
all day long.

WORDS YOU SHOULD KNOW

bark — the outer part of the trunk, branches, and roots of a tree

beak — mouth parts of a bird; bill

claw — the nail on the toe of an animal

clover (KLOH • ver) — a plant which has three leaflets

curious (KYUR • ee • us) — want to know or learn

dairy farm (DARE • ee FARM) — a farm where cows are raised and milked

grain (GRAYN) — the seed of the wheat, corn, rice, or other cereal plants

grind — to crush or pound into very small pieces

healthy (HEL • thee) — to be in good condition; to be normal

hen — a female chicken when fully grown

herding (HERD • ding) — to keep animals together; to gather

lawn mower (LAWN moh • er) — a grass cutter

pasture (PAST • chur) — land covered with grass and other plants that are eaten by animals

plow — a farm tool used to break up the soil

protect (proh • TEKT) — to keep safe; guard

quick (KWIHK) — fast

rooster (ROO • stir) — a male chicken when fully grown

swallow (SWAHL • oh) — to make food or liquid go from the mouth into the stomach

sweat (SWET) — a liquid that collects on the skin when you are hot

tiny (TIE • nee) — very, very small

tractor (TRAK • ter) — a machine used to pull other tools or machines

twig (TWIHG) — a small branch

INDEX

About the author

Karen Jacobsen is a graduate of the University of Connecticut and Syracuse University. She has been a teacher and is a writer. She has never lived on a farm but has visited many. Once she had a pet chicken, and now she has lots of plants.